Earth Has No Sorrow

By Beverly Moore-John

PublishAmerica
Baltimore

ISBN: 1-60474-076-0
PUBLISHED BY PUBLISHAMERICA, LLLP
www.publishamerica.com
Baltimore

Printed in the United States of America

To WTJ
my life with yours
gave me
words

To my Audrey and Amanda
the mystery of your womanhood
unfolds when you understand
your mother

PART I
SECRET UNIVERSE

In my secret universe
I stand alone
on the edge of darkness
and the word is spoken
then desire burns the blackness to light
and I write

Chapter one: innocence's repose

In innocent laughter and faith
I stepped into the world
and it received me

The Waiting Years

I'm here.
At the Door of Adulthood.
I stand here blinded by happy tears and filled with fear as I recollect the
memories of my life.

...wide-opened eyes to curiously explore the cold, strange world beyond my
mother's womb. crawling. walking. running. growing mysteriously and lovely.
learning right from wrong. learning the sad sounds of crying and the blissful
sound of laughing. spending hours away from home in school. learning to get
along with other people. learning to let go of a friendship that died away in its
sleep. discovering boys. hurting from the semi-sweet pains and pleasures of
school-girl crushes. experiencing a sweet relationship that grows with love.
realizing that my body has bloomed into an exposed flower for all the world
to see, but letting no touch. learning the fulfillment that comes with winning,
the discouragement that comes with losing, and the victory that comes in trying.
learning that life is not what I want it to be, but what I make it. learning to
make God first and last in everything...

Now, I've approached a door to the entry of adulthood.
I stand with mixed emotions.
I turn to see what I left behind.
If find nothing but the past.
I turn the knob of life.
I open the door.
I step inside and steal a shy glimpse of all the waiting years.

Solitude Undressed

Sometimes, I feel as though I am a piece of wood
drifting on the waters; finding my way in the
paths of a lonely ocean.
Floating aimlessly.
Feeling small and insignificant. Resting on the blue foaming
waters unnoticed.

But, then, I find myself embraced in the arms of a mighty wave
that places me tenderly on the shores of that once lonely ocean.

Someone touches me with the feelings in his eyes and makes me beautiful.

Needing You

I need time
 to hold you
 to feel you
 to taste you
I need time
 to talk
 to laugh
 to cry
 to mingle in your emotions
I need time
let us find time soon.

Lessons

I grew to love marriage and motherhood,
The feel of lovemaking and nursing.

I learned that many goals can be reached; many
cannot.

I understand, now, that working together means
working harder alone.

I am beginning to see love's cost.

Feeling Fine

Taking it easy

Feeling fine

Lying back

Spending time.

Taking it easy

My loves and me

Life seems almost

Problem free.

Your Guitars

Every time I hear your guitars,
I feel my younger sadness. That nagging
reminder of someone not caring enough.

Then you played; you strummed everything I longed
for. Your music unknowingly touched my insides
and made life peacefully bearable.

Every time I hear your guitars, my melancholy
soul is pierced. You touch me like no other.

Your music sings me complete.

I Cried

One night I cried hard, hesitant tears.

Tears of no emotion,
Tears of no pain,
Tears with no stirring in my soul.

One night I cried a bitter, truthful tear.

One night I cried, "Reality".

Soft Summer Nights

I remember soft summer nights.
Long talks
Kisses, never ending
Electric bodies clinging
Pure enjoyment
Good nights
Never ending good-byes
Kisses, never ending
I remember.
My body remembers.
And we enjoy the remembrance of…
I remember.
And I enjoy the remembrance.

Chapter two: for the children

You are the hope that moves life
But you are more than that
You are love reincarnated
You are the joy
and you are
always becoming.

Peering Out the Window

Two little girls
slender and tall
dignity wrapped in milk chocolate
ebony hair in second day cornrows.

Two little girls
standing outside
enjoying the gentle, early afternoon
breeze
they chatter rhythmically
they laugh with youthful ease
and someone knows
someday
two little girls will.

Sweet Baby Girl

I can hardly believe
when I looked in your eyes
for the first time
I met joy and love
unlike the genders
at passion
but radiant piercing soft
emotional love
and I felt I would open again
just for you, wonderful eyes
precious mouth
that cried
here am I
love me for a lifetime
I am yours

Almost Thirteen

To feel your confusion as you struggle to become
and find a place where you fit
To take a corner of the sky and say "this is mine;
this is where I belong."

To see you try in your girlish way
to crawl over obstacles
makes me long to cradle you as I once did
but instead
I stand by and
I push you, you say
So that someday you will realize an invisible,
knowing pull disguised itself so that you would
no longer crawl over obstacles—
but instead
use them as a podium to stand
and to realize that
a corner is no longer necessary because you can
claim the sky.

Still Lovable

At birth
lovable
At five
more lovable
At ten
most lovable
At fifteen
willful
defiant
stubborn
rude
know-it-all.
Fifteen and
still lovable.

Birth Not by Conception

You, who knew me before I lived
taught anger to fly
because
you walked where you
did not want me to go
and I determined
to wander where I will
stubborn girl
woman wise
you allowed me to happen.

You, the weaker vessel
who came full
and ripened
overflowed out of yourself
to rear eternity
mothering all
who would observe
your instincts pulled me
cautioned
encouraged
and saved me
your emotional logic
conceived
what you knew
would early become
woman.

Pain in the Motherhood

mommy watches
adorningly
curious
innocent
little child

mom watches
cautiously
assertive
willful
happy-go-lucky
teenager

mother watches
helplessly
hurting
struggling
determined
young adult

(and Someone knows
someday
two little girls will)

Beckoning

My children rise up
not to call me
Blessed
but to
call me out.
Imagine that!

Child's Play

hopscotch
double dutch
dodge ball
ring around the rosy
Mother May I
play
role reversal
so you can
dodge
emotional taunts

Contrasts

Back in the day
we had a way
of seeking
longer days...
coming to attention
in the presence
of Elders
falling silent
in disagreement
obeying without
apparent
hesitance
whenever we thought
our smaller sizes
to be wearing out
we were reminded of
the authoritative
shout
"I brought you into this world
and
I will
take you out."*

*This expression prevalent in the African-American community does not imply physical and emotional violence or child abuse; but rather speaks to the position of authority held by parents.

Training Wheels

Departing
home at
eighteen years
Destination
maturation
Arriving…

Yet

when i grow up
i want to be a butcher
and present the fatten calf
i want to be a baker
and cast my bread upon the waters
i want to be a candlestick maker
so a light on the hill
will
ever
burn
i want to seek
first the
Kingdom of God
and
i want to find
myself
in the courts of the King

Farewell

You came,
and crowned us
Granddaddy,
and endearingly called us
Grammy,
and permanently marked us
aunties and uncles.

You came,
unburdened
happy
and pure;
but this old world sharpened
its claws on you and darkened
your path
and weighed you down.

The secrets of your mind,
you held.
The pain in your life,
you harbored.
The confusion of your soul,
Someone understood.

The tragedy of your Being,
no one could conceive;
that you who made
us all firsts,
the Beginning of the Third
Generation,
would be the first to leave.

Journey well, our infant love.
Travel light this time.

Farewell to the boy child who left us sadly too soon. Rest.

Chapter three: also intimacy

When love is good
it speaks for itself
and it sings
in the voices of the
heavenly chorus
come to earth.

Lovers' Conversation

Look at me and like what you see
Be fascinated by me
Touch me with a lover's touch
Softly, urgently
Intentions made aware
And speak with me vulnerably
Knowing that I hold your words
As I hold your body in mine
Warmly, and completely absorbed.

Soulful Morn

I like our morning songs
as you pull me to you
your body finding me
and pivoting within
your guitar fingers touch me
and play rhythmic tones
tones that bring raindrops from
a hidden cloud
We sing our soulful rounds over and over
encouraging an ending
never in unison
but always in harmony

Chapter four: coming to terms

Shout.
Shout about who I am
Hear me if you can
Listen if you dare
it matters not how
you receive me
Shout
and talk all about me
I am something
to talk about.

Broken Heritage

no sense of place
the universe is my world,
but I haven't got a home.

BROKEN HERITAGE
my human soul battered
and denied, the greed of
wanting ghosts blood falsely
justified.
Oh…broken heritage!
Africa is Alive!!!
I will gather her pieces.
I will make her complete.

God & Me

Some people pray.
Others sing sweet, eloquent refrains.
Still, others may dance.
I prefer to love many things
for in loving many things,
I know God.

How do I find God?
By attending church? By examining the words
of a book? By vain repetitious prayers of others?

I think not.

I have found God by visiting the silence
of my yearning self.

By observing all the simplicities of life, I found
God inside myself; then I am no longer
afraid of being myself.

Nova

In my mind's eye, I see you
and I remember
strange adult tales
tales a child should not have consumed
but lives a child observed without
adopting.
I see you and I know the soul
of a woman is hidden by a safe silhouette
of life.
I know a beautiful spirit lies nestled
inside yearning to dance again.
When I see you, I see myself
and I realize, out of your pain came
me: a gentle woman clothed with tenacity
unyielding persistence and moxie.
I know
now
as I understood then
that a woman must never lose sight of her private
self.
May you embrace life and live as your spirit
leads.

Wholeness

I romance myself
not as my man does:
He wraps me with
soft savory touches, lending themselves
to hungry earthy movements
melodious raspy masculine voice
sending urgent messages
interpreted by my feminine ear
only
painted with visible whispers of his
pleasant appetite…
Freedom seduces me and
I pursue it
We connect
my body yields; eagerly wanting
opening with abandon
sweet fulfilling life giving
Explosion
Then, I find ultimate enjoyment in my man
and the way he romances me.

Woman Child

When a child cries in the night
salty waters flow from a
tender broken heart
unwilling to speak its pain
timid
afraid of what words will reveal

creaking floor boards
warm milk
securing arms
bring forth calming understanding
easy infant slumber

but when a child cries in the night
at thirty-one
she cries alone

Different Drummer's Diapason

I sing a startling song loudly in my soul
that no one hears; but the universe understands.
The score suits me; I am the score.
I leap in dance
I still in dance for
I am enchanted by the different drummer's rhythms.
They fill me up.
I dance and their romance is infused with my somber
embrace and I am affirmed.
I shall long love the different drummer
for I am she.
Criticism cannot assuage the rhythm within.

Propensity

A friend came to my life one year
and made me smile a smile
I had forgotten.

A friend came to my life one year
and made me realize again
the beauty that is me.

Agenda

Every now and then
my soul is frustrated
twirling round in sane insanity
and I wish you gone

Gone so my spirit may be alive uninterrupted
maybe than the circles will
straighten
and attempts made will
become goals achieved

Every now and then
sane insanity
urges me to love only myself.

The Threefold Cord

Always alone and hidden
sleepwalking through a
life of neglect and broken
promises of the threefold cord

No one knows how well
I am not
for I man the fortress
I steady the structure
I am a solid foundation
like my ancestors
the potential of others is realized
from my bleeding back

Try as I might
to preserve my being
Thrive if I dare
Life has determined to
undermine my sense and
break my spirit
I will not pay such a cost

Awaken, O Woman
and walk away with self
partnership begins within

I am the threefold cord
I am not easily broken.

Chapter five: women in thrive

In the family
we belong
the good and the bad
In the family
we see and
we tell the truth
about ourselves
and what is real
we see and
we don't wink
In the family
we are there
holding ourselves
together.

reeky blackness of opticians and bankers

in places of white opacity
blackness looms and
springs forward
in illuminating
truth
slicing into
glances,
tones,
and ill regard,
and
bounteous ignorance
affirming the spoken
and silent wisdom
of countless Elders
that blackness
from the outside
is always
a poor
evaluation

Sylvia

woman to the bone
wears it well
in vivid style
bold and sharp
flare undenied.

wrapped in alienation
undressed by validation
woman to the bone.

won't allow unraveling
well, maybe for a while
hurt over come by passion
then accessorized in
queenly fashion
and take the runway again.

Sylvia
woman
to the bone.

Define This

Everywhere I turn they want me to see
black and white
Everywhere I turn they want me to live
black and white
Everywhere I turn they want me to feel black
Yet everywhere I see hues all encompassing
mingling embracing mixtures of people
differences similarities singin' dancin' eatin'
having a good ol' time
courtships marriage making love families
babies crying
we cry, we hurt, we bleed
a transparent tear, a universal pain
the same life giving red blood
we laugh
you know the language
bilingual
everywhere I turn I see people; I see a person
I live a life; I feel feelings
I am humanity
So everywhere I turn
I refuse their offerings
and I will be who I am without their definitions

The Warrior

The nature of the warrior
to throw a flaming spear
and pierce the heart
mercilessly
and bring your mind to fear

The nature of the warrior
poised to strike deadly blow
the nature of the warrior
knows when to lay low

The warrior's speech did quiver
The warrior's face did quake
The warrior could have slain you
hatred a savoured mistake

No,
The Mighty has not fallen
The Powerful lay it down
and you will rightly witness
the Glory
of the thorny crown.

Just Like a Tree

like the rings of a tree
peer into me
and you will see
the catastrophes
I have endured

Recompensing

i was born
knowing
the suffering of
my people
i have seen
sad dewy
brown eyes
gleaming
questions
why? why? why?
i have long welcomed
tender timid embraces
unwilling to release
me
for fear and affection
i pay homage
to the history
i give honor
to my elders
I am born
knowing
the suffering of
my people
and
I live
knowing
my responsibility
for a victimless
existence

Rancor

I met hatred
face to face
and did not flinch
it engaged itself
in pompous exchange
it reasoned by
pigmentation
it reasoned by gender
it reasoned by
nationality
it reasoned religion
it reasoned by sexual
preference
it reasoned by political
affiliation
it reasoned itself to excuse
because all points of hatred
are moot.

Chapter six: painfully universal

and when it came to greet me
I knew it not
for the truth has
many faces.

Missed the Point

Coming at me.
Shocked paralysis.
Hit me full force.
Then journey on
and leave me hanging
heart and mind dangling
wondering
whether we survived
the moment
of impact.

Unloved in Conjugality

My heart deeply knows a pain so great
and dwelling
A large gaping sore that bleeds
profusely
spurting and spewing forth
when least expected
Drenching my soul
Oh Great Devine!
my heart aches monstrously
aches and breaks and dies daily
then is resurrected to a
loveless death so morbid
it struggles to live.

Soladad la Visita

Loneliness comes to visit
with me
like a long ago friend who
lost touch through time,
unwarranted.

Loneliness comes to visit
with me
and indulges me in slow motioned conversations
of loveless midnights.

Loneliness comes to visit
with me a while
and stays
and I lie in bed in sleepy longing and
welcome him
like a hungry lover feasting on
generous affection...
stay por favor.

Special

Even then
I heard it
in the rhythm of your voice
confidently disguised in Caribbean boast
Even then
I heard it
before it was ever said

Even then
I knew it
pride spilled from your eyes
responsibility bore a badge of honor
paternity undenied
Even then
I knew it
after I misunderstood

Even now
I hear it though it's seldom said
Even now
I know it though it's seldom shown
Even now
it holds me
when I'm weeping to the bone.

The Disappearance of Love

absent glances
eyes meet only in anger
biting words repeating
repeating hurting lingering refrains of
unreal expectations, disappointments, and
skewed perspectives
absent tender thoughts
absent loving touches
present unshared bed
the quiet mystery of the night
once enjoyed together now
dreaded alone
fears imagined
real
and growing throughout the years
of marriage

Ar-gu-men-tum

Words connote feelings
void of esteem, attacks of personhood
While slivers of moxie, pride
glisten in mind
taunting and teasing
daring
the heart of judgment to uprise
daring
the heart of pain of prevail
words connote
but cannot define
the heart of love
and its redemption

Birthdate

Tall
Thin
Happy go
Lucky
Confident
Kind
Know where I
Want to go and
How to get
There
Transformed
to sorely and
blatantly unloved

Question
How far will you go
before you realize that
you hate yourself
and then you hated me

Anger

I never thought
the heart that
reached out and
soothed my soul
would claw and coil
in bitter biting clenched
anger
and craft my
life's death

Chapter seven: spiritually spirited

I have got a life
to get happy about
it writes
me
everyday
as God whispers
in my ear.

Resilient, Resilience, Resiliency

Heartaches
sex
and
snakes
just when
you find what fits
they change their skins
and quit
being useful
oh well...
what the hell

A Conversation Between Friends

"Come, ye disconsolate."
I heard a whisper say
I lent an ear momentarily but
then I turned away.

"Here bring your wounded hearts."
the whisper turned to plea
I walked toward the sound of it
but oh, my heart did flee.

"Here tell your anguish."
my Lord cried out to me
and I in helpless surrender
reached out my hand to Thee.

I gave you, God
an account of years
and shed the cleansing tears
and you listened
no judgment, no rule
no ridicule.

I rested there
in Divinity's care
my lighten soul made real
the promise of the Living Word
*"Earth has no sorrow that heaven
cannot heal."*

In My Bones

Talent sashays in
and claims
the kisses of the passionate who
cannot not do it
It stirs up Spirituals
and bellows Blues
It grips the Gospel
Amen
Talent swings on Jazz
and lingers on the Count, the Duke, and
the Lady
Philosophical, poetic Reggae
make I and I know
we talented big
Rocked and Rolled
Rhythm wedded Blues
It's all Soul, it's all soul
Talent
sashaying in and
loving the passionate
who cannot
not do it.

Mommy Ain't Crazy

Mommy
if you did not
write
you'ld be crazy

Mommy if you did not
laugh
robustly
through stinging tears
you'ld be crazy

Mommy
if you did not
dance
like music's
in your soul
you'ld be crazy

Mommy
if you did not
sing
your gospels
spirituals and hymns
you'ld be crazy

Mommy
if you did not
pray
you'ld be
crazy

Write me to disclosure
Laugh me to ease
Dance me to intimacy
Sing me to release
Pray me to peace

Mommy if *you* did not
we would all be crazy
we would be crazy
Pray me to peace and
Write another poem

Chapter eight: *full circle*

It was but a little that I passed from them,
but I found him whom my soul loveth.
I held him, and would not let him go...[1]

Now I Lay Me

Remembering when
sleep massaged my mind
at the end of day
as I lay
beneath open window curtained breeze
lulled
of play and chores
and Worship
into a resting place
of quiet babies
nestled
at mothers' breasts.

It Is You

Let affection roam
travel my heart
journey my soul
I know your first
presence
it lingers long after
familiarity met acquaintance
It is you
who made me
to know
the first love of life
and the life of love
It is you with whom
I share the Promised Land.

Chapter nine: working

In the Office

I saw my future
entirely:
painful humiliations
degradations and
rejections
I saw the house divided against itself
It did not stand.

In the Office
I tasted
entirely
the cup of professional
curses
that would not be taken from me.

In the office
I realized
entirely
that the perceptions and dreams
were real
and positioned myself
to run.

In the Office
I saw
a man
of authority and compassion
move on my behalf
bewildered
like a frightened doe

I ran and ran
exhausted
running on empty
believing all was well
except me.

In the Office
i made partnership
with the God of
my childhood.
In the Office
i do His bidding
and He reminds me that
i am fine.

Three Tears of Anger

Within my eyes
waterfalls
of
humiliation
degradation
and rejection
instruct me.

Within my eyes
water falls
and I cannot consent to
witness
another's drowning.

Within my eyes
waterfalls
create
three tears of anger
and I
throw out a lifeline.

Chapter ten: a time to cast away stones

Changing

Who can explain
uselessness
when children
can do by themselves
and husband redefines
manhood?

Wife and motherhood
no longer understood.

Reconstruct.
Create womanhood, personhood
for yourself and
become what you choose to be.

A Deceived Heart

in the company of men
rambunctious brag, shaken dice
and lady luck kissed hand
Lucifer whispers
like a man
"gamble,
you will not surely die."²
in the company of men
rambunctious brag, count a lay
and prove your worth
you can't beat my score
a real man has more than one
"All these things will I give thee, if
thou wilt fall…"³
in the company of men
a man loses
his soul
his life
his wife

Not Quite Death

So many years
trying
but not minding
the effort
because my heart
said, "love is worthwhile."
So sad
when all tumbled
down and
ended
in divorce.

Necessary EXPRESSION

Can it be said that the masculine cannot cry?

Can it be said that the strong cannot be weakened?

Well, it's alright to shed a tear.
It's alright to feel.
It's alright to show a hurt.
It's the way to live.

Can it be said that the feminine will cry?

Can it be said that the weak cannot be strong?

Well, it's alright to hold it in.
It's alright to be firm.
It's alright to hold some pain.
It's the only way we learn.

The Freedom Process

Freedom
beheld
awakens my life
and unleashes
the real me

What the Dead Do

Contemplate
what it is to live
and laugh and embrace
until satisfaction
determines
I am alive

Tears over Tea

a sob lingered inside us
at your request
intact
unwilling to release a
truth
that could have saved four of us
now, I cry
tears over tea
the Truth has set me
free
to say good-bye
Heaven holds a door that
easily leads to a friend
if you care to walk in
you can hold my hand
again
and be who you are

Prayer of Compassion

If I could have prayed you to peace,
I have done so.
If I can pray you to peace,
I will do so.
Pray you to peace,
I do so.

....desire burns the darkness to light and I write.

PART II
LOVE CONQUERS ALL

"...and at our gates *are* all manner of pleasant *fruits*, new and old, *which* I have laid up for thee, O my beloved."[4]

A: A Fondness Between Us

The Beholder's Eyes

A painted portrait hung
lonely
on the wall
in a crowd of faces
lonely
eyes searching
wandering
roaming
galleries of curiously quiet
awe struck admirers
a painted portrait hung
lonely
on the wall
coyly emitting
soft feminine radiance
wondering which
beholder's eyes
she would find
beautiful

Propensity

A friend came to my life one year
And made me smile a smile
I had forgotten.

A friend came to my life one year
And made me realize again
The beauty that is me.

Revealed

I viewed your face
and met might and insecurity.
I read your eyes
and felt your longing.
I listened to your voice
and heard youthful tenderness.
I have yet to feel your touch.
I know not your love.
And I wait to know you...
and I wait
to know
you.

Angel by My Mailbox

dear whom it has concerned
your message reached
you make me smile a smile
I cannot forget
for I still feel your loving
eyes adorning me
it is pure complementary
fondness,
this propensity

bring your message
directly
you have reached me.

A Curious Affinity

"Let him kiss me with the kisses of
his mouth: for thy love is better than wine.
Pleasing is the fragrance of your perfumes;
your name is like perfume poured out.
No wonder the maidens love you!
Dark am I, yet lovely,"

except

"…they made me take care of the vineyards: my own vineyard I have
neglected."

Even so,

"the king hath brought me into
his chambers.
Tell me, O thou…"[5]

of this curious affinity.

Playful Giggles

Today, three little girls
me, myself, and I
full of happy-go-lucky
mischief
giggled and laughed
and blushed
and giggled and giggled
and kept a secret going
because we realized
a
supreme
temptation.

Colourful Pleasure

He likes
soft springtime green
beautiful
exuberant
vibrant
ever-blooming
me.

In Agreement

You are near
but I want you here
beside me
besides
you want it
too

My King

Come see the eyes that adore you.
Know the soul that believes
you are of a sweet, regal persuasion.
My body waits to receive you
and my heart yearns to love you.

Security Blanket

Woven threads
human and angelic
draped me
to health
like a Linus blanket
around
a Charlie Brown Christmas tree
living strands of kindness
your active compassion
restored my hope
now, the desire cometh
and it is a tree of life
Thank you

Enticing

I am having fun
again
and I would like to
share it with you.
I hope we are looking forward
to
friendship
companionship
partnership
and...
(you let me know)
if all goes well
you may whisper in my ear
and call me your baby.

Date Talk

Today was easy and pleasant.
A bit of comfort came my way.
I thought of you today, as always.
It is delightful how you are like the
air I breathe, ever-present, unseen,
necessary.
How are you, sweetie? How was your day?
Is there anything that I can kiss away?
Think of me tonight before you slumber.
I have soft, cool feet that you
alone can warm.
Goodnight.
I'll see you in the morning.

Date Talk

How are you, sweetie? Are you well?
Tonight before you slumber remember,
it is I who will lie beside you
and give you a sweet lullaby.
Remember, too
that you are my morning glory
and I am your trumpeter.

Do you know what I want?
Masculine and feminine laughter
and talk of nothing in particular,
easy comfort,
and you.

Goodnight, sweetie.
I'll see you in the morning.

Wanted

Have you ever wanted to walk about town
holding hands, talking, or take a
country drive in silent comfort?

Just being with you is enough to
fire spontaneous kisses, tender
passionate embraces, and easy laughter.

Have you ever wanted to slumber at
midnight, spooning, and wake to
see the morn together while
I respond
as you rise
to greet me?

Vulnerable Today

the lady needs strong arms
to drape her
and hold her
just hold her
for eternity
as if she were
the only precious
flower on earth.

Console Me

sometimes
I want to
lay my soul
on your pillow
and cry
myself to sleep
in your comfort.

For You

For you I cry a tear of
imagined passion.
For you my daydreams linger and
my night dreams plead.
For you I wander and wonder when
we will meet.
For you I remember a smile I had forgotten.
For you acquaintance is not enough.
For you my night dreams plead.
For you, I wait.

The State of Affairs Tonight

Crying
to sleep
in my sleep
tossing and
turning
finding
no one beside
me
to kiss away
a tear.

Unfulfilled Longings

Remembering to forget you
is not easy,
for God reminds me that
He has fitly joined us
in Eden;
and He will have His way
regardless of my stubborn and
impatient heart.

Something's Missing

The five a.m.
silence
reminds me of
when it was
not so silent
at five a.m.

A Song's Dream

I see you
in my dreams
with me
swaying
to a soft
sexy
sensual
song
I see you
in my dreams
with me
and I hold you
in my heart

Silver Tongue

Promise me
what you will
and I will lie
enraptured
and encourage
you to make
good
your word

Advertence

In my life
and in my
love is excellence
nothing short of
God-centeredness
within
fruits of the Spirit
active, maintained,
and sustained
personally
individually
together
He has taught lest
I forget
the deception and
my willingness to endure
His lessons and His grace
are forever joined in me
As much as I know we
can love
As much as I now we
can play
As much as I know we
can work a life
Without the main ingredient,
I walk away.

Horizons

Clearly,
from a distance,
heaven and earth
meet
beautifully.
Near,
heaven and earth,
are
one.

clearly
from a distance
heaven and
earth
meet
beautifully
near
heaven and earth
are one

Abidance

I think of you
I think of you
All I ever do is
think of you.

And I know that
I love you.

So, I'll wait for you
to show me why.

Yes

Ah, I hear him—my lover!
Here he comes, leaping on the
Mountains and bounding over the
Hills. My lover is like a swift
Gazella or a young deer.

My lover said to me, 'Rise up, my
Beloved, my fair one, and come away.
For the winter is past, and the
Rain is over and gone. The flowers
Are springing up, and the time of
Singing birds has come, even the
Cooing of turtledoves. The fig trees
Are budding and the grapevines are
In blossom. How delicious they
Smell! Yes, spring is here! Arise,
My beloved, my fair one, and
Come away."[6]

Let's Get It On

The presentation is done.
The introductions have been made.
Do not dot every "i" and cross
Every "t".
You have already provided a security
I have never known.
Let's get familiar together.
Let's become common.
Let's make it real.
Let's get it on.

Affinity

Touch me once
Touch me twice
Take me all the way
to paradise.

Touch me once
Touch me twice
Make me smile
and declare you
nice.

Marriage

blessed heart
blessed body
his love
truth and
undefiled passion
sing a joyful morn
touching me
artfully *dolce*
as if he has
a rival
because
he knows
he has not.

Punctilio

Immaculate
Conception
gots nothin' on
Unanimous consummation
Con amore

For My Beloved

Make haste to have me slowly
calm not passion's flame
thy touch has ever consumed me
thy love goeth down sweetly.
Make haste to love me slowly
lie tenderly at my breasts
thy lips receive willing companions
thy love goeth down sweetly.
Make haste to have me slowly
savour a full release
thy longings enjoyed my caresses
our love goeth down sweetly.
Make haste
to love me slowly
our love goeth down, sweetly.

Body Language

Night speaks in blue black
cool whispers,
compelling the secret visits of
passion not consummated.
Talk. Talk to me,
slowly warm your words by the
heat of my breasts.
Simmer down some sweet pillow
talk lavishly drizzled over my
sweat silken body.
Night speaks in white-hot purring
utterances.
Talk. Talk to me.
Quicken me.
Hastily send your words on
silver tongue to the place where
we communicate.
Umm...do you hear me listening?
Talk, baby. Talk to me.
Night speaks and we like
what it's talking about.

One Guardian

At the union
of my thighs,
is heaven.
Come
home.

Variety at the Honey Altar

At the altar
you are man
and I am woman.
Enjoy your desires with me
and we will indulge.
Affection is pleasurable
because you are skillful and
I am willing.
In your private presence this lady is
first a woman.
Come.
The marriage bed is undefiled, come.

Succumb

You came
to me in a dream
a complete man
masculine and gentle
bringing for me
your urgent love
to rescue
my captured femininity
and unchain my soul
so that you could
move freely
within me
You came
and made all the
difference

Again

In your private presence,
I whisper softly
the words of love.
In your private presence,
I dance at the
touch of your music.
In your private presence,
I call your name
as you kiss the
insides of my thighs.
In your private presence,
I delight in our enjoyment
because in your private presence
this lady is first
a woman.

always.

Declaration

No words
describe
no feelings
explore
what God
has joined
and made known.

B: Hurt

Subsided

If everything that I say
means something that
I do not mean
then
I will not cling
I will not give you
a place in my heart
and
I will not give your body
purpose in mine.

What You Say?

Women say
don't love a man
too much
I say
don't love him
at all.

You heard me!

Two Sides of the Side Coin

love and playfulness
love and commitment
love and marriage
love and indifference
love and anger
willingness and effort
press on

Little Foxes

You have taken
tender moments
and reduced them
to a
false definition.

Familiarity

Sometimes
when we make love
his mind is preoccupied
and I do not
feel him.

Frankly Speaking

One moon lit starry night,
courted.
One glorious day,
joined
in Eden's paradise.
One time in our bedroom,
the honeymoon
ended.

Friction

Touch me the way
persistence feels defiance
Show me how your
continuously smooth moves
handle my unruly sultry
dispositions
Teach me why
sugar and spice
make love
extraordinary

Truce

Taking peace
in the valley
and moving
to higher ground.

PART III
CRAZY AFTERMATH

Ignominy's Blessing

Humiliated?
yes.
Disconcerted?
perhaps.
Shamed?
guilty.
REDEEMED
Absolutely.

Fishbowl

Doing the best I can
and yet remains
reports of
bitter heart
ill health
and contrived situations
of *concern?*
meant to
motivate me to
scurry about
and accept the unacceptable.
will I never
be relieved of
this curious
surveillance?

Lava

quiet.
like an untroubled
nonchalant garden brook
in calm repose
flowing flowing flowing
to an assured destination
silent.
and the rock cries out.

Undone

I live alone
by myself
a lonely
undeserved
solitudinarian
is there any
wonder
that
my sodden
peculiarities
would usher
foul
play?

RENT

Severed.
Disjointed.
Rejected.
Tossed out.
Lost.
Wandering....
and
Finding myself
by myself
in a most lonely hostile
place.

Soulful Lamentation

Isolation
breeds
hunger
a tremendous rumble
that besieges my body
causing pain
that sends me
running frantically
salivating
and panting
searching for that
soul food plate
of social encouragement

Reprieve

Halted along my homeward journey,
I stood still
to watch the whirlwind.
I covered not my head,
but
boldly participated
from the eye of the storm.

Rivers in the Desert

Cry the tears
of heaven
upon my soul
my heart withers
in anguish
flow down
sweet healing
waters
the basin of my being
is as parched
crackling desert
cry the tears
of heaven
upon my soul
make my spirit
like new earth
kissed by morning's dew.

Answered Prayer

You took the
words of my mouth
and the
meditation of my heart
and made them
acceptable
in your sight.

Thank you.

Enabled Disability

Slow-motioned thoughts
frustrated anger
propelled
a body to run.
unconquerable obstacle course
quickened a spirit
to soar, determinedly.
quiet
regal
unembellished
acceptance
of impedance
befriended her purposes
to be content
only
with excellence.

Inaudible

Silent.

And dead.
Watch how I say it.
Individually speaking,
Can you hear
me
not talking?

Nia

My purpose in writing
is to speak
a truthful
powerfully
refreshing
gentle
rainstorm
that unexpectedly
captures
my raging hot
melting soul
and
nourishes me
to new growth

-Ing

No working
income
No sassy
haircut
exercising my beauty
and an enemy
within
is taking seed
rooting
and growing

Sidebar-Ing

work
exercise
take
root
grow

TICKED! PISSED! VEXED!

Seconds turn
to minutes
tick tock
tick tock
ticked
wanting to rid
myself of polluted
waters given to
nourish me
pissed
let the waters fall
cleanse me
of vexatious
well intended
rabbi
vex
me for the
last time
DISMISSED!

Lessons from Rabbi

Sleeping dogs
lie
for good reason
they are resting
preparing for an
awakening

I.
conflict left
unattended
runs a life amuck

II.
conflict
wisely managed
reaps a person much

Guilty

I have said things untrue, perhaps
made mistakes for sure
and maintained lies
from forgetfulness
or remorse
repentance
and forgiveness
others from
pride and stubbornness
declaring
ain't no body's business
all seems well
but then in an
instant
my conscience
who is no respecter
of persons
asserts herself within
and beats me
'til Kingdom come.

Introspection

the truth hurts
and it has not
set me free

A Tangled Web

This confusion
serves me right
all that they know
they do not know
all that they think
is not so
I am caught
in the mayhem
of sinister minds
weaving

Voyeurism

soap operas
are real
for a privileged? few
their sudsy blues
were not meant to be
sung by the rest of us
they permit us
voyeurism
hot scenes in our
lukewarm lives
tantalizing and teasing
painting the town red
and leaving dreg
turning our whites
pink in the process
and we wear them
still

Inspiration

Something happens
inside of me
mind, heart, and soul
disturbances
words turning
churning
mingling and mixing
regurgitating poetry
exhausting me

Malaise

A long momentary anger
flashes within
it grips my attention
it probes my mind
it ponders, pesters, and
instigates fracas
between repose and me
and instantly
renders
my life incomprehensible.

Throw!

This time
I did not
send things
Clashing!
Banging!
Splattering!
against the walls
This time
I wrote a poem.

Pain in the Motherhood

mommy watches
adorningly
curious
innocent
little child

mom watches
cautiously
assertive
willful
happy-go-lucky
teenager

mother watches
helplessly
hurting
struggling
determined
young adult

(and Someone knows
someday
two little girls will)

Separation

With expert parting
i brought you into my world
of cozy hand-made love
with amateurish parting
i gave you to
a world unfamiliar
to me...a home
i did not make...
a place with no
refrigerator stick people drawings
or crayon colored green skies
and blue grass
with sadden eyes
i speak of feelings
whose acquaintance
i am displeased to acknowledge
through tearful sighs
i extend a reluctant hand
to regret and loneliness

Blues

silent eleven o'clocks
near midnight
indigo
sea
sky

Funny Reasoning

strange imaginings
turned
outside
in.

Accented Enunciation

The voice
has elements
of every
utterance
and
every
sound
judgment
simply
unobtrusive
magnificence
that expresses
every
dialect

Uncultured

He pays
attention
to every
prayer
to every
prayer
spoken in faith
for His Eyes
see
with His Heart
every
prayer

Carte Blanche

Life visits me
camouflage in humour
uttering sentences
incognita
wisdom and folly
in the same place
I at times
will grant her
polite audience
mostly I give
sassy retorts
pin-pointing her
facetiousness
life insists on
visiting me
camouflaged in humour
and I cannot ignore her
for who am I
without her

Innocence

One day I saw a woman
with all of her
complexities and
complications
laughing
a gleeful
jolly belly
laugh
and the voice
of her own
merriment
transported her grown up
mind
to a child's heart.

Struggling

I do not mind
people knowing
I've got problems
and no solutions
that Spirit speaks
and I hear
happenings
and
see sounds
I do not mind
my mind not being
mine
because a time ago
I gave it to the
Great Divine

Recovery

Listen,
he said no
emotional connection
he said it
plainly,
I hear it
plainly.
Understand?

Okay, All Right, All Ready

psychic, no
clairvoyant, perhaps
but primarily
a Child of God
my address is
2468 Pearly Gates
so there is no need
to hang a shingle on
the corner of 9th
and the 1-800
number is not
my number

Name Change

Beverly Moore
Given
Beverly John
Chosen
Beaver
Endearment
Bev
Approachable
Bevie
Fondness
Beverly Moore-John
Reconciliation
Beverly
Me

A Day in a Life

Making it real
Keeping it real
Being real
that's life

Crazy Aftermath

When crazy people
get it together
Zs
come before
Ys
and ain't
nobody
asking
how it came
2b

PART IV
TENDER LOVING CARE

In Sickness

if I could
detach the
attachment
to survival
I would
walk
off the face
of the earth
I am terminally
loving
in chronic pain
and in need
of mercy

And in Health

Someone's
attention
affection
and
compassionate
acts
walked before
me to the cliff
and prevented
my undoing

Colourful Pleasure

He likes
soft springtime green
beautiful
exuberant
vibrant
ever-blooming
me.

Love Becomes the Rose

Complement
extends
generosity
to Lonely Heart
despised
for
single-mindedness

Reap

Confidently
studying to do
my own business
and making As
even after
failing
marriage
101.

Attainment

If this is all
there is
it is all
there is
given me
graciously
It is mine
and I am
thankful
it is all

Converse

Cocooned in a rain-washed
meadow of wildflower dreams,
I emerge fluttering to
listen to butterflies whisper
my past, present, and future.
Rain-washed wildflower dreams
live refreshed and
they invite me to treasure
a rainbow that is given me.

Home

I have traveled the universe
mindward
I have touched heaven
in a dream
I have experienced earth
indescribably
hell visited
once
twice
once, twice
and I walked away
to a place
where you are
always able
to reach me

Finale

My reality is not a dream.
My dream
is
a
certain
reality.

PART V
I WILL SING

His Hand

a comforting
place of
power
and of peace
piercing
the soul of a
wounded spirit
and making me
whole

Identity 1975

I am yours; you are mine.
Why can't our thoughts entwine?

I am of your womb; your blood flows through me.
Why can't I think as you and
You think as me?

The answer is:

Though we are one, we are two.
You can't be me and
I can't be you.

With You in Mind

Though the years and reasons have
Torn us apart,
I hold immeasurable love for you still.

Though our opinions differ,
I love you still.

Though I grew up despite your rejections,
I love you still.

Though your traditions are not my traditions,
I love you still.

You will always come to mind because,
I love you so.

To my mother, December 1982

Honey

The man I call Daddy
does not know
of a daughter's
love and admiration.

He has not experienced
tender caresses and
soft humorous kisses
created after a daughterly fashion.

He does not know that she
secretly studied and copied
him and
understandingly
disregarded
imperfections.

The man I call Daddy
is no longer the epitome
of manliness
seen through
delighted ten-year old eyes.

But if he wanted to be,
he could be.

To my father, December 1982

Sabbath

calling	calling
calling	calling
calling	calling
Voices	Voices
of pure	of pure
quiet whispering	quiet whispering
wind	wind
calling	calling
calling	calling
calling	calling
Spirit	Spirit
heartbeat	heartbeat
Hallelujah	Hallelujah
Hallelujah	Hallelujah
Hallelujah	Hallelujah
from	from
the highest	the highest
mountain	mountain
to the	to the
lowest	lowest
valley	valley
Excellence is	Excellence is
summoned	summoned
because	because
God	God
is speaking	is speaking

Unfinished Business

Squarely
once
you told
that my
principals
would not
tolerate me
they have
saddened you
and
I know it

Fruitful

I've got a half penny.
I've got a red cent
and two cents worth of
no thing
that everyone conspires
to take.
I offer the contents
of my heart
but the gleaning of my bones
satisfy.

Avoided Gait

Through my neighborhood
I walk
straight back
and breathe
the
atmosphere

Through my community
I stand
to look around
and see
the
connection

Through my family
I live
enlivened
to feel
the
light of day
and to know that
I am
not a
throw away

Nine Months Told

sisters and brothers
know teenage life
mothers quietly
observe
fathers patrol
friends and neighbors
tell generations' old
tales
and all families
hold secrets
that are not
secrets

Everyone's Opinion

How can I
pretend
to be the lady
that I am

WORD

If you plan
to compete
you must have
something more
than envy.

Our Elders

They sang
Humble me, humble me
and let me do thy will
They sang
It's me, It's me, It's me
Oh Lord standing in the
need of prayer
They sang
When we all get to heaven
I sing
and I know
that we make
the best
of life on earth
mistakes and all

One Flow

I do not wish
to remember my days
of tender youth
before my eyes opened
and I tasted the world
without permission.

I wish not to ponder
conditions, circumstances
consequences, and rewards.

I understand they exist.

I wish only to live
my mid autumn knowing that
fallen leaves are nourishment
and I am forgiven.

PART VI
HALLELUJAH'S TOLL

Mable Lee Harris Moore
in loving memory
1936 - 2001

You are already sorely missed.

Cradle to the Grave

Now
i
lay me
down to sleep
i
pray
the LORD my soul
to
keep
ifishoulddiebeforeiwakeipray
I AM
in my mother's arms

Forgive Us Our Debts

Sooner than later
the Creditor
calls
to collect

Amends

paid
in
full

Mother's Womb

dear mommy
first and seventh
gather 'round
second and fifth and sixth
talk
third sits laughing
at the foot
of the bed
daddy
is at the door
and Lisa is in the cradle
thank you mommy
love from all of us

Part VII
Upon Mine
High Places

Remembering

Realizing
that liabilities
exceed assets
and income is
a meaningless word
understanding that bills
are always due but
never met
watching how vehicles become
unreliable when needed most
sympathizing with appliances
because they are old, tired,
and used.
Remembering Mommy and
Daddy and
knowing that I have
built a life not
worth remembering.

Sorrowful Ways

exist
because
all has ended
before it has
begun

Her Story

Winter's steely touch
no longer chills my soul
because I permit
him to warm
his hands
upon my heart

and never miss a beat

Appointment

disappointment
is
not as bad as
it seems
it helps to resolve
the irresolvable
disappointment
is not as bad as it seems
it simply
feels
unseemly

Virtue and Praise

In my loneliness
and verge of
chronic despair
a heart with
a voice
reminds me
of things true
such as love
of things honest
like a baby's kiss
of things pure
like quiet morning worship
of things lovely
like a Philippians chapter four thought
of things of good report
like perfect recall
of wonderful memories

Inaccessible

Don't want
to see the
Light of Day
because it may
reveal that my
Heart's Desire
is just
a stone's
throw away

Unfaithful

After I have
given my heart
body
and
much
to be with
you who
are not God
What does it
profit me?

Obloquy

wonderful face
glowing smile
bright eyes
observing all
finding beauty
and knowing
abuse

*This poem is a result of mental illness—a very strange emotional and mental trauma that I cannot fully understand to this day. It is not a result of abuse in my marriage.

Even though the fig trees have no blossoms, and there are no grapes on the vine; even though the olive crop fails, and the fields lie empty and barren; even though the flocks die in the fields, and the cattle barns are empty, yet I will rejoice in the LORD! I will be joyful in the God of my salvation.[8]

PART VIII
RUEFULLY ON

Divorce is worse than death; the mantra is rejection.

A: Economics

Crying

I do not know how
to face
this world
a woman alone
and make it
I do not know
how to become
economically
successful
and remain
Heaven bound
I do not know
how to remove
my soul
like tight fitting
shoes from tired
swollen feet
and lay it down
to rest

Call Center Customer Service

working hard
but hardly working
enough
to get paid
so maybe
I'll try
Getting laid
EXPENSIVELY

Unemployed

Wisdom crieth
chastity!
chastity!
and other
virtues
Wisdom crieth
and
she is unmarketable
and so
attractive

Scented Seconds

Come
take a
whiff
while the saliva
of another man
drips
from my lips.

Majora minora

Vulva
Clitoris
Vagina
why do you
separate
legend
from the
Woman
and expect
her to *not*
advertise
what is
most
desirous

Mockery Thought Out

her husband
praises
the Proverbs 31
woman
only after
his thirsts
have been
quenched
by many cisterns

Asunder

phraseological
verse
wedding
vows

B: Competition

Perspective

God
would have it
that life
is
conception
creation
and birth
naturally speaking
Earth is
a woman's world
with manly assists

Exchange Rate

men and women
want what
I've got
because I am
happy
and my soul
is not for sell

Responsibility

Emulous Cupidity
left simple heaven
for complicated hell
because
love said,
enter through
the front door
and remove your shoes
but lust
left the back door
open
duty free

Implications

working hard
but hardly working
enough
to get paid
so you all
are suggesting
I get laid,

Too EXPENSIVE.

C: Harmed

Self-Hatred

paired melons atop
soft used pillow, resting
once protrusion
now, flatten wide
engulfed by jerk
pimple rind
stealthy persuading
me to become
a parade float
controversy
uncelebrated
with plenty
unnecessary sustenance
and the mirror gloats

Struggle's Boredom

a different day
a same night
a different same day
a same night
a same different day
a same night
a different day
a same night
a different same day
a same night
a same different day
a same night
a different day
      a
      same
      night

Misdiagnoses

The doctors say
they
have names and treatments
for what I am experiencing.

I say, so do I.
It's life.
It's situational.
And my coping mechanisms
Are fine.

Illness

King David, Job, Mrs. Job,
Hannah, and me.
I've got no income.
No work. No job.
No nothing but
a soul.
O, to use
the fish and loaves
to feed the
multitude of needs that
crowd my life.
If *The Physician* proclaims,
"chronic, acute, serious",
who am I to deny
the diagnoses, halt
a benefit and delay
the remedy?
King David, Job, Mrs. Job,
Hannah, and me.

PART IX
HEALING BALM

Prologue

Seeing my scar
and
knowing
that I
have it
and why
bothers me

Mariah's Vulnerability[9]

Speaking
communicating
gives another the
right
to decide early
dishonesty
is easy

Antiseptic Niagara

something's
left inside
the song
cannot
release it

I would cry
if I died
before
love kissed me.
I would go
to my grave
mournful of life
with remembrances
of eyes that once
touched my soul,
knowing the voice
never whispered
in my ear.
I would cry
if I died
before
love kissed me
I would cry
tears.

Landing

I do not
want to die
alone
I want to die
with love
beside me
in bed
soothing my head
kissing my face
bidding farewell
ushering eternal
day

Whispered Well

I would cry
if I died
before
love kissed me
Song of Songs.
I would go
to my grave
mournful of life
with remembrances
of eyes that once
touched my soul,
knowing the voice
never whispered
in my ear.
I would cry
if I died
before
love kissed me
Song of Songs.
I would cry
tears.

Verbalism

Laughing now
at the folly
of my extreme
romantic imaginative
prose.
I would die
if I cried
for a love affair
virtually
experienced.

God Technology

Power-pointed
transparencies
reveal
everlasting
horizons

Lullaby

I am a woman
passed young
and precious infant
voices sway cradled from
lofty weeping willows
that do not weep
rather smile billowing
blanket softness.
I am a woman
passed young
enough to know
that when the wind
blows moonlit starry nights
cerulean waves touch
you and me to life.

The Sound Outside

The chirping birds
do not compete
with the lyrical wind
and branches
orchestrating leafy melodies
Nature's concert
is harmonious
when the heavens sing

Impromptu Scripture

Sitting at his feet
learning my words
and writing.
O, to be a writ
like The Psalmist!
I wish to pray
like Solomon,
"Give thy servant an
understanding heart..."[10]
I want to be greatly beloved
like Daniel,
"At the beginning of thy supplications
the commandment came forth..."[11]
When a child,
I held you in
fond curiosity.
I knew you existed.
You were my
constant companion,
innate guidance and
a strong right hand.
Then, in young womanhood,
I realized surely
you answer prayer.
I thought,
yes, we are partners!
Wrong was I.
Partners? Later, I understood.
You are Saviour,
I am saved

by *your* grace.
Sitting at your feet
learning more than my words
and writing—
learning how to live
your way.

Storytelling

I wrote my life
with memories of girlhood
in the backyard
off the kitchen
under a crabapple tree:
my head a mist by
a sudden spring rain
refreshed senses indulged
with fragrant heaven scents
and earthen warmth in cooling.
Father gave me his resemblance,
Mother bequeathed her heart
of experiences then,
I scribed my life in
my bedroom
canopied by reflections
of myriad others.
A time ago hurts
past,
eyes peaked anger to
misinterpret cleansing expressions
imprinted in severance.
I wrote my life and
my life writes me.

Peace

I hear the real
universe
again
he speaks nicely
as if he is
my friend

PART X
MIXED MESSAGES?

New Games

yin yang appointments
flirt freely
because the time is ripe
and she feels
like it.

Black Widow and Octopus

Seven

Do You Feel Like Fun Now?

you make an arrangement
we will socialize
can we talk and
laugh and hang out
together
you decide
it's
up
to
you.

Eager

My bam is for looking
not touching
I am saving it
for paramount love
It is mine
I twist it
shake it
roll it
You have a little joy
I move along
alone

It is widely known that the feminine body brings enjoyment to the masculine eye. Men of diverse cultures are particularly fond of women with abundant buttocks.

A woman, who is a lady, manages responses by presenting herself discreetly.

Eager speaks to the delicate art of pursuit and interest. Ideally, a man pursues and a woman, if interested, declares her level of approachability. The woman's preferences must be honored.

PART XI
PASSIONATE FEMININITY

Unchained Femininity

invites
a man
with oos and ahhs
and softly
wiggled hips
she kisses to please
because he pleases her
and she does
his waltz
with assured
pleasure
expertly

Market Day

I need baskets for my melons
baskets for my melons
the lunar moon wheels
their pulp is laden
substantially
come
explore the pith
baskets for my *melons*
baskets for *my* melons
your two
will do
nicely

Dwellan

washing dishes
in the kitchen
scrubbing floors
in the bath
wiping dust
from old furniture
and walls
can you see me
when I am disheveled
can you want
to kiss my lips
when they speak
the truth
can you want to
love me
when I appear
unlovable
wiping dust
from old furniture
and old walls
can you make me
your dwelling place

PMS

Please
make
sense
my emotional logic
is inclusive
your stoic logic
exhausts definition

Precious Ointment

sweet quiet beauty
is serene, compliant
and alluring
send evil to court
her and she will
place rose petals
at your feet
and bury you
with the light on

Discourse

arrectis auribus
ars est celare artem

arrivederci

With ears pricked up:
Attentively.
It is true art
to conceal art.

Till we meet again,
Farewell.

Afterword

People say the sincerest form of flattery is imitation. I say, the most sincere compliment is thank you.

Today, I am surviving and thriving. It is not of independence but interdependence. I am a product of a People:

From my parents, brothers and sisters, friends and acquaintances, the church of my childhood and the church of my adulthood, the schools I attended, to a colourful, vibrant community of relatives, in-laws, neighbors, and strangers.

In many hands, God placed me.

Thank you to you all. Your words and your works made a difference.

A Word Regarding Mental Illness

Sometimes, it just takes time. And that's okay. We all cannot just get over it or snap out of it. Sometimes, it takes medication, counseling, prayer, self-appreciation, respite, and time.

For information regarding mental illness visit:

National Alliance on Mental Illness (NAMI) at www.nami.org
Mental Health America (MHA) at www.nmha.org

Endnotes

1. Solomon 3:4 KJV

2. Genesis 3: 4 KJV

3. Matthew 4:9 KJV

4. Solomon 7:13 KJV

5. Solomon 1 KJV

6. Song of Songs 2:8, 10-13 NLT

7. Psalms 19:14 KJV

8. Habakkuk 3:17-18 NLT

9. Muse: If It's Over, Emotions, Mariah Carey—Cole/Clivill s Music Enterprises

10. 1 Kings 3:9 KJV

11. Daniel 9:23 KJV